# The Cata[strophe]

## THE GREATEST SHOW

# ON EARTH

### Written by
### Kate Scott

### Illustrated by
### Tom Bonson

Published by Pearson Education Limited, Edinburgh Gate, Harlow, Essex, CM20 2JE.

www.pearsonschools.co.uk

Text © Kate Scott 2013

Designed by Jo Samways
Original illustrations © Pearson Education Limited 2013
Illustrated by Tom Bonson, Advocate.
Cover design by Tom Bonson and Jo Samways

The right of Kate Scott to be identified as author of this work has been asserted by her in
accordance with the Copyright, Designs and Patents Act 1988.

First published 2013

17
10 9 8 7 6 5 4 3

British Library Cataloguing in Publication Data
A catalogue record for this book is available from the British Library

ISBN 978 0 435 14369 5

Printed and bound in China by Golden Cup

Acknowledgements
We would like to thank Bangor Central Integrated Primary School, Northern Ireland; Bishop
Henderson Church of England Primary School, Somerset; Bletchingdon Parochial Church of
England Primary School, Oxfordshire; Brookside Community Primary School, Somerset; Bude
Park Primary School, Hull; Carisbrooke Church of England Primary School, Isle of Wight;
Cheddington Combined School, Buckinghamshire; Dair House Independent School,
Buckinghamshire; Glebe Infant School, Gloucestershire; Henley Green Primary School, Coventry;
Lovelace Primary School, Surrey; Our Lady of Peace Junior School, Slough; Tackley Church of
England Primary School, Oxfordshire; and Twyford Church of England School, Buckinghamshire
for their invaluable help in the development and trialling of the Bug Club resources.

Every effort has been made to contact copyright holders of material reproduced in this book.
Any omissions will be rectified in subsequent printings if notice is given to the publishers.

# CONTENTS

# Chapter One

"Ouch!" Tess yelped as something small and hard bounced off the top of her head. A small, dark pellet fell onto the hard dirt next to her.

She sighed and strode across the yard. The chickens squawked and flapped, alarmed by her shouting. The cow, the horses and Stub the mule were still in the barn. From the racket they were making, it sounded as if they hadn't been fed yet. Tess shook her head.

If Ma caught Jim idle again, he'd be in big trouble, and when Ma got mad, she could holler the ranch down. Luckily for Jim, right now Ma was up to her elbows in a washtub of hot water, scrubbing the week's laundry on the washboard. But if Ma found him before Tess did, her brother would be in more trouble than a cowboy with a snake bite.

Jim's dog trotted up to Tess. "Where's Jim, Bullseye?" Tess gave a gentle tug to one of the mongrel's ears. "Where's he hiding?"

Bullseye licked her hand and led her to the wooden fence that separated the yard from the rest of the ranch's land. Tess slung her legs over the bars of the fence and hopped down to the other side. Bullseye went down on his belly and wiggled under the lowest wooden slat to join her.

Tess found her brother crouched down behind a bale of hay that Pa had left the day before. "Jim!" she hissed. "Why haven't you done your chores?"

Jim's fingers slipped and the pellet from his catapult went flying. There was another loud squawk as it hit one of the chickens.

"Oops," Jim said. He tipped his face up to his sister and grinned. "Got to practise, Sis. She's going to be here any day now!"

"*Who's* going to be here any day?"

Jim stared at his sister. "Annie Oakley – the best catapult shooter in the West! She's in Buffalo Bill's travelling show and it's coming to Lizard's Lick!" He held up his catapult. "They say she can hit fifty clay pigeons in a row. Bang, bang, bang – just like that! And when Buffalo Bill throws a card up in the air twenty feet away, Annie can punch a hole right through it."

Tess frowned. "So why does that mean you have to practise *your* catapulting?"

Jim put another pellet in his catapult. He took careful aim at a stack of tin cans and let the sling go. The pellet soared up into the air – in the opposite direction to the cans – and hit one of the fence slats. The pellet bounded off the fence and hit Bullseye right on the nose. Bullseye let out a reproachful yelp and slinked back behind Tess for protection.

"Sorry, fella," Jim told his dog. "I've just got to practise a little bit more."

He turned to his sister. "After the show, they let people from the audience come up and show what they can do. If I can prove to them that I'm a great shot and a good rider, they'll invite me to join them in the show."

"But, Jim ..." Tess didn't want to upset her brother, but she couldn't lie to him. "You're *not* a great shot."

"Not yet," Jim said, grinning. "But I will be."

He picked up another pellet and took aim at the stack of cans. This time, the pellet knocked a tile off the barn roof.

"You see? That was close!" Jim grinned at his sister. "When I get into the show, I'll be earning good money," he went on. "I'll be able to buy Pa a new pair of cowboy boots, and a new wood stove for the kitchen, and a new horse ..."

Tess shook her head. Her brother's stubborn cheerfulness was one of the reasons she loved him but, if he catapulted at the show like he just had, everyone would laugh him out of the ring. The thought of the whole town of Lizard's Lick laughing and pointing at Jim sent shivers down her back.

"First things first," she told Jim. "I'll help you get the chores done before Ma comes out and hollers at you for being idle all morning. Then I'll help you practise your catapulting and riding.

You won't be getting into any show if you keep hitting dogs and chickens. Not to mention your sister."

"Thanks, Sis!" Jim tucked his catapult into his breeches. "I'll make you proud at the show, you'll see."

As soon as Jim had put his catapult away, Bullseye trotted straight to his side. Tess smiled. Jim had a special way with dogs and could make Bullseye do anything – except go near him when he was shooting with his catapult.

Tess followed her brother back into the yard. To make Jim a good enough shot with his catapult to impress Annie Oakley wasn't just going to take practice; it was going to take a miracle!

# Chapter Two

Tess and Jim saddled up and rode down to the creek. It was about a mile away from the ranch, so Tess figured it was safer to do their catapult training down there. If Jim kept causing havoc at home with his poor shooting, Ma might ban his catapult altogether. Though Tess couldn't help wondering if that would be such a bad idea.

Tess was riding her piebald pony, Banjo. Next to her Jim rode his mule, Stub, who was snorting grumpily.

Jim reached forward and patted Stub's neck. Stub shook his mane, stopped in his tracks and twisted around to give Jim a filthy look. Tess laughed.

"That old mule's meaner than a rat bite," she said.

"Aw, he's all right," Jim said. "He's just a bit slow to warm up, that's all." Tess smiled. Pa said that Stub was the most grizzly, stubborn mule ever born and you needed a prairie full of patience to ride him. That's why he'd been given

to Jim. Pa said Jim was like an apple in water – no matter how many times you pushed him down, he kept on bobbing right up again.

"Hey, boy, on your feet!" Jim called to Bullseye. Bullseye stood up on his hind legs and tottered along for a few steps.

"You taught him another trick!" Tess said. "I don't know why you want to bother learning to shoot straight when you're so good at training dogs. You could train every dog in Lizard's Lick!"

*Maybe if I can convince him*, thought Tess, *then he'll finally give up on this whole being-in-the-show dream.*

"But that wouldn't mean working with Annie Oakley, Tess," Jim said. "She shoots so straight she could knock the tail feathers off a rooster." A starry look came into his eyes. "Can you imagine what it would be like to shoot alongside Annie and Buffalo Bill? With all those people watching and cheering?"

Tess sighed. It looked like she wasn't going to be able to change Jim's mind. Instead she was going to have to try and teach Jim how to shoot straight.

They pulled up next to the creek and tied Banjo and Stub to a tree stump.

"Let's go over to that clearing where it's quiet," said Tess. There was no need to tell Jim she wanted to get far enough away so the animals wouldn't get hurt.

Jim pulled out his catapult. Bullseye turned and started to slink over to join the pony and mule.

"Hey, come back, Bullseye," Jim called. "I'm going to need you."

Bullseye whimpered and gave Stub and Banjo a longing look, before turning to follow Jim as he walked towards the clearing.

"The first thing is to choose your target," said Tess.

Jim pointed straight ahead. "How about that hickory nut hanging on that branch over there?"

Tess looked at the tiny nut hanging from a tree far in the distance. She shook her head. She had to hand it to her brother – he sure was confident.

"Let's start with something a little bit easier," she told him. *Like something that's possible*, she thought.

Jim shrugged. "Whatever you say, Sis."

Tess picked up a large stone from the side of the creek. She walked up to a nearby tree and put the stone on one of the lower branches.

"There," she said. "We'll start by using that as a target."

"Great!" Jim put a pellet in his catapult and raised his arm. Bullseye immediately darted behind one of the trees.

"Wait a minute!" Tess put her hand on Jim's arm to bring it down. "I'm supposed to be giving you some pointers, remember?"

"Oh yeah, sure," Jim said.

Tess took her catapult and a small, dark pellet out of her pocket. "You release the sling early if you want your shot to travel high and short. You release it late if you want it to go long."

"Early for short, late for long," repeated Jim, nodding.

Tess took aim and let go. Her pellet soared through the air and knocked the stone clean off the branch she'd put it on. She walked over and replaced it. "Right. Now you try."

"Annie Oakley, here I come!" Jim raised his arm and pulled his sling back. His pellet shot out in the opposite direction to the tree branch and landed with a loud *thwack* next to Bullseye. Bullseye jumped about three feet into the air. Then he scooted over to Tess, keeping low to the ground.

"I hit something!"

"Yeah, just not what you were supposed to hit," Tess said, but under her breath to save her brother's feelings.

But Jim was already running over to the undergrowth to see what he'd hit. "Hey Sis! I scared off a snake!"

"Well done. You probably saved Bullseye from a nasty bite," Tess said.

"I knew you'd get me up to scratch for the show." Jim beamed. "If I can shoot a snake I must be ready. Let's do the riding tricks now."

Before Tess could take a breath to reply, Jim had taken off towards Stub. By the time she'd caught up with him, he was already mounted.

Stub did not look happy to have his afternoon snack of grass interrupted, and glared at Tess as she untied Banjo. Tess sighed. She thought trying to teach Jim riding tricks on the most obstinate mule in town was a waste of time, but when she looked at Jim's face beaming down at her, she knew she had to try.

Half an hour later, she had tried to lead Jim through walking Stub backwards, quick turns and jumping over a log – and Stub had refused to do any of it.

Tess could see that the mule had had enough. There was a glint in his eye that Tess didn't like the look of.

"I think we'd better call it a day, Jim," Tess said. "Pa was right. You can't teach a mule new tricks. Or in Stub's case, even old ones."

"Aw, please, Sis; let me have just one more try," Jim pleaded. "If I can show Annie and Bill that I'm not just good at catapulting but good at riding too, they'll have me in their show quicker than a tick on a dog's back."

Tess thought this was about as likely as Stub standing up on his two hind legs and doing a jig, but she didn't want to upset Jim. She sighed. "If you're sure." She glanced over at Stub, who still had a face like thunder. "Then let's try the jump again."

Jim nodded and gave Stub a jab in the sides. "Come on, fella, up!"

Stub snorted once and then started to move forward.

"That's it, here we go!" Jim shouted.

Stub cantered forward a few feet and then bucked wildly, throwing Jim to the ground with a loud *thump*.

Tess ran up to Jim. "Are you okay?"

Jim sat up, breathing hard, but smiling. "I'm fine. Stub's probably a little nervous. I'm sure he'll be great tomorrow."

Tess stared at her brother. She'd been hoping that practising would either make Jim better at catapulting and riding or – even better – convince him of the truth: he would never, *ever* be any good at either of them.

How was she going to prove to him that performing in Annie Oakley's show was going to be a disaster?

# Chapter Three

The next morning, Ma and Pa told Jim
and Tess they could ride into town as
soon as their morning chores were done.
Jim was whistling as he mucked out the
horses and led them out to the corral.
He couldn't wait. But as Tess milked the
cows and swept the yard she felt nerves
wiggle like worms in her stomach. *What
was going to happen at the show?*

Three hours later, Jim and Tess finally arrived in town. They tied up Stub and Banjo and made their way to the bull ring in the town centre, where a huge banner announced the arrival of "The Amazing Buffalo Bill and Annie Oakley". Bullseye, who had followed them into town, trailed along just behind. Wooden benches had been set up all around the edges of the ring. Some of the riders for the show were spreading sawdust, ready for the shooters and riders to perform on.

THE AMAZING BUFFALO BILL AND ANNIE OAKLEY

Jim and Tess handed over fifty cents each for their tickets to a cowboy with a bushy moustache. He wore a wide-brimmed hat tipped back on his head and smiled down at them as he handed them their tickets.

"Enjoy the show," he told them.

"I will – I'm going to be in it after today," Jim said, grinning.

"That so?" The cowboy looked Jim up and down, a small smile lifting the corner of his lip.

Jim nodded, his grin widening. "Look forward to working with you, partner."

The cowboy slapped his thigh and roared with laughter. "Look forward to – ah, that's funny, kid. That's real funny."

He clapped Jim on the shoulder, still chortling. "I'll keep an eye out for you at the end of the show."

"Thanks!" Jim followed Tess as she led them to a space on one of the benches near the front of the ring. "Hear that, Sis? He's going to keep an eye out for me. These fellas are going to be great to work with."

"Yeah, that's good," Tess muttered. She glanced behind them and saw the cowboy standing next to Wes Black from the Lizard's Lick Store, pointing over to them with a grin.

Tess felt her face flame. Everyone in Lizard's Lick had always liked her brother. She couldn't bear the thought of everyone starting to laugh at him.

And that wasn't the only worry – there was every chance that Jim could hurt something with his catapult – and this time it might not be a snake. Bullseye must have been thinking the same thing because he crouched down low to the ground between them, letting out the occasional pitiful whine.

She was about to try again to convince Jim not to volunteer to perform at the end of the show, when a horn blasted and the master of ceremonies strode out from the tent at one edge of the ring. He was taller even than Pa, and was wearing an enormous white hat with a bright red handkerchief tied around his neck.

"WELCOME!" He roared. "WELCOME ALL IN LIZARD'S LICK ... TO THE GREATEST SHOW ON EARTH!"

"They'll be out any minute!" Jim whispered in Tess's ear. "Annie Oakley and Buffalo Bill!"

Tess decided there was no point worrying yet.

Maybe Jim would see how crazy his notion of joining the show was, after he'd seen the standard of their shooting.

"AND NOW," the man hollered. "INTRODUCING … THE AMAZING, THE INCREDIBLE … THE SHARPEST CATAPULT SHOOTER IN THE WORLD … ANNIE OAKLEY!"

The crowd clapped enthusiastically, some slapping their knees, as Annie Oakley appeared on a huge grey horse and cantered around the ring.

The next moment she was up on her feet, balancing on the back of her horse. She plucked a catapult from her pocket and held it up as the crowd cheered. Buffalo Bill appeared, holding a sack. He pulled a handful of clay pigeons from the sack and started to throw them up in the air, one after the other.

Bang! Bang! Bang! The clay pigeons shattered into tiny pieces in mid-air. Jim leapt to his feet and whooped.

"Go, Annie!"

Bang! Bang! Bang! The crowd started counting – seven, eight, nine, ten!

Annie Oakley continued to shoot from the back of her horse.

Eleven, twelve, thirteen!

Buffalo Bill slung them up high, faster and faster.

Fourteen, fifteen, sixteen, seventeen!

The clay pigeons barely had the chance to get up in the air before Annie Oakley's arm brought them down.

Eighteen, nineteen, twenty!

By the time Annie had got to forty, the crowd were on their feet, roaring.

Forty-eight, forty-nine, FIFTY! Annie Oakley held both hands up in triumph as she pushed her horse to a gallop and careered around the ring.

"She did it! She catapulted fifty pigeons!" Jim jumped up with excitement, his eyes sparkling. "She's amazing, Tess!"

Tess was grinning too – she understood now why Jim had fallen in love with the idea of the show – you could almost taste the excitement in the air.

The rest of the show passed in a blur. The riders did some breath-taking tricks – jumping from one horse to another with some of the show's chickens perched on each shoulder and held under each arm, jumping over log piles five feet high, and galloping around the ring at a pace that set the audience's hearts racing. Buffalo Bill and Annie

Oakley catapulted at a series of targets while everyone cheered them on. By the end, Jim and Tess had almost shouted themselves hoarse.

At last, the master of ceremonies came into the centre of the ring.

"PEOPLE OF LIZARD'S LICK, YOU HAVE WITNESSED THE GREATEST CATAPULT SHOOTING IN THE WORLD. NOW ONLY ONE QUESTION REMAINS – IS THERE ANYONE IN THE AUDIENCE WILLING TO PIT THEIR SKILL AGAINST THESE MASTERS?"

As the crowd waited to see who would volunteer, Tess whispered to Jim, "Don't do it, Jim, don't do it." For a moment, Jim hesitated, looking out at the ring. Tess held her breath. *Had her brother seen sense?*

But then Jim shot up, his hand high in the air, and called out. "I'll do it; I'm in!"

"THEN COME ON DOWN, BOY! COME ON DOWN!"

Tess's stomach plummeted. He'd done it. All that was left now was to wait for the disaster …

# Chapter Four

Jim wasn't the only member of the audience to make his way down to the ring. A man who looked to be their Grandpa's age had also stuck up his hand. He had a red spotted neckerchief around his neck and wore a battered old hat pulled low over his face. His huge grey bushy beard came down almost to his waist.

The master of ceremonies gestured to the man with the battered hat. "AGE BEFORE BEAUTY!" he cried, as the audience laughed.

Annie Oakley and Buffalo Bill stood by, as some of the riders set up a pyramid of tin cans and a flag pole with a clay pigeon on top. The old man stepped forward and aimed his catapult. His pellet hit the tin at the top of the pyramid and toppled it. He slowly took aim and fired – another tin fell. He paused, and looked around. There was a spatter of unenthusiastic applause.

He raised his arm again and shot down one more tin. He shuffled his feet as he prepared to take his next shot.

The audience became restless and started to mutter. After the fast-shooting of Annie and Bill, the older man's methodical manner was too slow to hold anyone's attention. By the time he'd hit two more tins, some of the crowd had started to boo.

*In a moment, they might be booing Jim,* Tess thought. Her stomach dropped into her boots.

The master of ceremonies stepped in as the older man went to take his next shot.

"THANK YOU FOR YOUR FINE WORK, MISTER. NOW LET'S GIVE THE NEXT VOLUNTEER A CHANCE."

The man with the battered hat frowned, but shuffled out of the ring obediently.

"NOW LET'S SEE WHAT YOU CAN DO, YOUNG COWBOY," yelled the master of ceremonies. Jim walked forward and whispered something to him. The man nodded and tipped his white hat.

"THIS YOUNG FELLA HERE WANTS TO SHOW US WHAT HE CAN DO ... ON HIS MULE! SO PUT YOUR HANDS TOGETHER FOR THE BOY!"

The crowd cheered as Jim ran off and a minute later came riding back on Stub.

Bullseye crept closer to Tess as Jim waved and walked Stub around the ring.

He pulled up in front of the pyramid of cans, which had been re-set up by the riders. He pulled out his catapult.

Tess held her breath. As Annie Oakley and Buffalo Bill looked on from each side of the pyramid, she had to bite her tongue to stop herself from shouting out a warning.

Jim took aim.

Maybe Jim would remember her pointers. Maybe he'd actually hit the target. Jim released the sling and his pellet soared through the air, knocking off Annie Oakley's hat with a *thwack*!

Maybe not.

Annie Oakley laughed along with the crowd as she picked up her hat from the ground. Buffalo Bill laughed too, but Tess noticed he took a step back as Jim tried again.

*Thwack!*

Buffalo Bill's hat flew off his head.

This time the crowd roared. Jim was proving to be just as entertaining as Annie Oakley!

Jim had one more try at taking a shot at the pyramid of tins – this time shooting the master of ceremonies' hat right off!  The pyramid remained completely intact.

Now Jim tried to put Stub through his paces. He urged Stub forward into a canter, but every few feet Stub stopped, his legs splayed out, until Jim managed to coax him forward again.

Eventually Jim decided to give up and took out his catapult again. The master of ceremonies, Annie Oakley and Buffalo Bill all made a great show of holding up their arms to shield their faces and the audience roared with laughter.

Tess looked over at Jim's face to see how he was taking it, but he was grinning from ear to ear. He lifted up his catapult and took aim at the clay pigeon on the pole. This time the pellet bounced on the ground at an angle and sent one of the show's chickens squawking. The pellet soared high up in the air, coming back towards Jim and Stub. Stub started backing up, but he wasn't quick enough – it hit him smack in the nose. Stub took off at a gallop, looking for a way out.

Jim tried to pull him back and Stub reared up, flinging Jim from his saddle and onto the sawdust of the ring.

The crowd roared again.

Jim quickly stood up, but before he could get back onto Stub, the master of ceremonies came over and put a hand on his arm.

"LET'S HEAR IT FOR THE YOUNG COWBOY, FOLKS! DIDN'T HE GIVE US A GOOD SHOW?"

The crowd leaped to their feet and cheered as Jim led Stub out of the ring. A few minutes later he re-appeared to join Tess.

"Can you believe it, Tess? They loved it! It went even better than I thought it would!"

"You don't mind about not hitting the targets?"

"I took their hats off! That's even *better* than hitting the targets!"

The man who had given them their tickets for the show strode up. "Hey, there. Thanks for the show. That was definitely worth keeping an eye out for." He caught Tess's eye and winked, smiling. It wasn't a mean smile, but Tess knew he wasn't saying that Jim had been *good*; he was saying he'd been *funny*. Luckily Jim didn't seem to notice he was teasing.

"Thanks!" Jim said.

Tess shook her head. If Jim thought it had gone well and the audience had enjoyed it, then maybe it was all right after all. She smiled.

But now she realised Jim wasn't moving along with the rest of the audience as they started to make their way out. She nudged him. "We should be getting home. Ma and Pa will be needing us for the chores."

Jim swivelled towards her and stared. "Hold on, Sis - I've got to wait for Annie and Bill. They're going to want to ask me to join the show."

*Uh-oh*, thought Tess. It clearly wasn't over yet …

# Chapter Five

Tess and Jim waited patiently as the rest of the audience made their way out, some stopping to slap Jim's shoulder and congratulate him on his "mighty funny show". Jim beamed, waiting confidently for Annie and Bill to re-appear. Tess wondered how she could make a last ditch attempt to convince Jim that his dream was never going to come true.

Eventually, the last of the audience disappeared and the riders in the show came out to sweep up the sawdust and dismantle the benches.

"I think I see her!" Jim said, pointing at the far side of the ring where the pyramid of cans had been set up. Annie Oakley, now dressed in a plain dark blue dress, was helping to clear the cans, tossing them into a large sack, while Buffalo Bill rounded up the chickens into crates. Jim waved, but Annie Oakley didn't seem to see him. Tess wondered if she was *pretending* not to see him.

"Maybe she doesn't realise I'm here," Jim said. Before Tess could stop him, Jim had put his hands to his mouth and was hollering, "Hi there, Ms Oakley!"

Annie Oakley looked up and gave a brief wave. Then she turned back to her job, finished up and walked quickly over to where a series of wagons had drawn up, ready to be loaded.

"Maybe she's waiting for Buffalo Bill to finish loading the chickens," Jim said, "so they can ask me together."

Buffalo Bill finished loading the chickens, then helped one of the riders lift a bench and carry it out of the ring. He didn't even look at Jim.

"Maybe they just don't have any room in the show at the moment, Jim," Tess said. She had to find a way to let him down gently so that he wouldn't feel miserable.

Bullseye crept closer to Jim's side. Jim bent down and ruffled the top of his head. "Good boy," he said, his eyes still fixed to the side of the ring where Annie and Bill were now handing up the last few crates of chickens onto the wagon nearest to them.

"I guess they're not going to ask," Jim said, his voice flat.

Tess squeezed his arm. "Well, what would we have done on the ranch without you if they had?"

Jim gave her a weak smile and sighed. "I guess we'd better head on home."

"Those cows aren't going to milk themselves," Tess said, trying to sound bright and happy, as if Jim wasn't looking like a lonesome puppy.

They walked to the edge of the ring to watch as the line of wagons started to move away. Bullseye trotted along at Jim's heels. As the last wagon left the ring, it rolled over a rock in the road and suddenly started to lean to the side.

Jim and Tess both watched in horror as the wagon wobbled and the crates of chickens fell from the back into the road. The crates smashed open and dozens of squawking chickens were freed. They ran in all directions, some escaping into the ring where Annie Oakley and Buffalo Bill had performed.

"Our chickens!" Annie Oakley appeared by the wagon, having jumped down from the one in front. The cackling chickens were scattering far and wide. "We'll never get to our next show on time now!"

"Don't worry, Ms Oakley," Jim said. "I can get your chickens back if you can get some new crates ready."

Annie Oakley frowned at Jim. "Really?" she said, doubtfully.

"Sure," Jim said. "Bullseye and I will take care of them in no time."

Tess smiled. At last Annie Oakley was going to see something Jim *could* do.

Annie Oakley waved over some riders and asked them to bring some more crates as Jim turned to Bullseye. "Ready, boy?" Bullseye wagged his tail and gave a soft "woof".

Jim gave a long, piercing whistle.
Immediately Bullseye took off after the
chickens in the ring.

"He's going to chase them further
away!" Annie Oakley cried out.

"Just wait and see," Tess told her.
"Jim's amazing with dogs."

Annie Oakley looked doubtful. Tess
held her tongue. *Jim and Bullseye
will soon show her!*

Jim gave two short whistles, followed by another long one. Bullseye changed direction and started running around the chickens, forcing them to draw closer together. Tess and Annie Oakley watched as Jim whistled commands and Bullseye darted left and right, bringing the tight pack of chickens closer and closer to the wagons. Annie Oakley started flinging the crate doors open.

"He's really going to do it!"

The chickens hustled into the crates, one after another. In a matter of minutes, the last one had been safely shut away. Tess smiled. Jim might not be able to shoot a catapult, but he sure could direct a dog!

Annie Oakley held out her hand to Jim. "Thanks so much for your help," she said. "You're my hero!"

Jim shook her hand, a grin spreading across his face. "No problem," he said.

"We'd better be getting on the road,"
Annie said. "We really don't want to be
late for our next show."

Jim's face fell a little as she started to
walk away. Then Annie Oakley stopped
and turned back. She pulled out her
catapult and held it out. "Hey, Jim, can I
give you this as a thank you?" Jim's face
broke into a beaming smile.

"You mean it?" Jim stared down at
the catapult.

"Sure. You might find it useful when you practise." Annie Oakley smiled as Jim took it and she gave a half-wink to Tess. "Show us what you can do with it the next time we come to Lizard's Lick."

"I will – thanks!" Jim grasped the catapult tightly in his hand, as if it might suddenly disappear.

Annie Oakley waved as she hopped back up into her wagon. Jim, Tess and Bullseye watched as the trail of wagons snaked out of sight.

"I knew it, Tess," Jim said, his eyes shining. "She loved my shooting! She said I was her hero! They're going to ask me to join them the next time they come through Lizard's Lick!"

Tess opened her mouth to argue and then shut it again. Maybe Annie Oakley's catapult would improve Jim's shooting. Maybe they really would come back to Lizard's Lick one day and ask him to join the show.

Maybe miracles really could happen.